Feathers and Wings, Beaks and Bills

James Frances

Momentum
Feathers and Wings, Beaks and Bills

First published in Great Britain in 1998 by

Folens Publishers
Albert House
Apex Business Centre
Boscombe Road
Dunstable
Beds LU5 4RL

© 1998 Momentum developed by Barrie Publishing Pty Limited
89 High St, Kew, Vic 3101, Australia
Reprinted 2000

British Library Cataloguing in Publication Data.
A Catalogue record for this book is available from the British Library

ISBN 1 86202 389 1

Designed by Pauline McClenahan
Printed in Singapore by PH Productions Pte Ltd

Every effort has been made to contact the owners of the photographs in this book. Where this has not been possible, we invite the owners of the copyright to notify the publishers.

A.N.T. Photo Library/G.D. Anderson p. 13; A.N.T. Photo Library/Bill Bachman pp. 6, 12; A.N.T. Photo Library/Jack Cameron p. 6; A.N.T. Photo Library/Brian Chudleigh pp. 16, 19, 22; A.N.T. Photo Library/Brian J. Coates p. 4; A.N.T. Photo Library/Martin Harvey pp. 7, 11; A.N.T. Photo Library/Gerard Lacz p. 14; A.N.T. Photo Library/Fredy Mercay p. 18; A.N.T. Photo Library/N.H.P.A. cover, p. 10; A.N.T. Photo Library/Denis & Theresa O'Byrne p. 9; A.N.T. Photo Library/Fred Park p. 19; A.N.T. Photo Library/M. Price p. 20; A.N.T. Photo Library/Otto Rogge p. 10; A.N.T. Photo Library/M.F. Soper p. 15; A.N.T. Photo Library/Dave Watts p. 13; A.N.T. Photo Library/Cyril Webster p. 11; A.N.T. Photo Library/D. Whitford. p. 21; A.N.T. Photo Library/Norbert Wu pp. 6, 15, 17; B. Silkstone pp. 4, 5, 7, 10; Ken Stepnell cover, pp. 1, 4, 8, 9, 16, 18, 19, 21; Bill Thomas p. 8.

Contents

What Do Birds Look Like?

All birds have feathers on their bodies.

Feathers help birds fly and keep warm. They help them hide from predators. They help them find mates.

Birds preen their feathers. This means they look after them by cleaning them and spreading oil through them. The oil helps keep the feathers waterproof.

A bird has two wings and a tail. Most birds use their wings to fly. They steer mainly with their tails. Wings and tails of different shapes help birds move in different ways.

Swallows catch insects in the air. Some have long, forked tails to help them change direction quickly.

Frigate birds fly long distances. Their long, pointed wings help them do this with slow, easy wing beats.

Birds have two legs and two feet. Most birds have four toes on each foot. The legs and feet differ in length and shape to suit what the bird does to gather food.

Wading birds have long legs. Sparrows have short legs. Many swimming and diving birds have webbed feet.

Birds do not have teeth. They use their bills or beaks as feeding tools. The bills and beaks differ in shape to suit the food the bird eats.

Hummingbirds eat nectar and insects. They have long, pointed beaks. Hornbills eat fruit and small animals. Their beaks are powerful.

What Do Birds Eat?

Some birds eat seeds and fruit. Some birds eat meat. Other birds eat insects.

Seagulls and crows eat almost anything. They are called scavengers.

All birds need water. Most birds get water by drinking. Some birds get all the water they need from the food they eat.

Where Do Birds Live?

Birds live all over the world. They live in forests and on wetlands. They live on grasslands and on tops of mountains. They live in deserts and in cities.

Many birds live together in large flocks or colonies. Others live as part of a small group. A few kinds of birds spend most of their lives on their own. Some birds are kept as pets by people.

Some birds stay in one place most of the time.

Jacanas only live on lagoons where water lilies grow. They walk across the lily pads in search of food.

Some birds travel halfway around the world each year. They breed in cooler places in the summer. They travel to warmer places in the winter, where there is more food.

Most swallows fly long distances across country. Shearwaters and rainbow bee-eaters fly over the seas.

How Do Birds Move?

Most birds can fly. They have strong, light bodies to make flying easier. Many of their bones are hollow. A large breastbone and strong muscles support their wings.

Some birds cannot fly. Emus and ostriches walk or run along the ground. Penguins live most of their lives in the water. They are excellent swimmers.

How Do Birds Find Mates?

Birds need to find mates at the start of the nesting season. They do this in various ways. Many male birds have bright feathers. They use them to try to attract a female. Male song thrushes attract females with a beautiful song.

Some birds do a courtship dance in front of the female. The peacock does this. Other birds build a spectacular nest, or bower.

Once they pick a mate, some birds stay together for life.

How Do Birds Care for Their Young?

All birds lay eggs. Some birds build nests to hold their eggs. They sit on their eggs to provide warmth so the young inside the eggs can grow and develop.

Nests can be found in trees and on cliffs.
They are often seen on buildings and in
hollows and burrows. They are also found
among reeds and grasses, or even on the bare
ground.

Sometimes, the parent birds take turns sitting on the eggs. Sometimes, the female or the male bird does this task alone.

In Antarctica, the male emperor penguin stands on the ice with a single egg on his feet under a flap of skin. He keeps the egg warm for 60 days, until it hatches.

The mallee fowl builds a mound to keep its eggs warm. The mound is made of sand and decaying leaves and grass. As the leaves and grass decay, heat is produced. The female mallee fowl lays her eggs in a hole in the mound. The male covers them up.

Some cuckoos lay their eggs in the nests of other birds.

Baby birds are always hungry. Sometimes, just one of the parents feeds and looks after the young. Sometimes, the parents take turns. Some have many family helpers.

The birds leave the nest when they can look after themselves. It will soon be their turn to find mates and begin families.

Glossary

bower   a shelter built of twigs by the male bird to attract the female

lagoons   shallow lakes or ponds

predators   those animals that hunt other animals for food

scavengers   animals that eat any food that is decaying or abandoned

Index